IN THE PUB

MW01280326

The Life and Work of

Regional Planning Pioneer

Ladislas Segoe

(1894–1983)

Published on occasion of exhibition

Organized and Published by the
College of Design, Architecture, Art and Planning [D A A P]
University of Cincinnati

With the generous support of the
Ladislas and Vilma Segoe
Family Foundation

EXHIBITION ACKNOWLEDGMENTS

PROJECT TEAM

Curation
David J. Edelman
School of Planning

Jennifer Krivikas
Robert A. Deshon & Karl J. Schlachter Library
for Design, Architecture, Art & Planning

Vincent Sansalone
School of Architecture and Interior Design

Jennifer M. Latessa
School of Planning

Design
Exhibition
Vincent Sansalone
School of Architecture and Interior Design

Catalog
Todd Timney
School of Design

Authorship
David J. Edelman
School of Planning

PUBLISHED BY

College of Design, Architecture, Art
and Planning [D A A P]
University of Cincinnati
5470 Aronoff Center
PO Box 210016
Cincinnati, Ohio 45221-0016
USA
tel: +(513) 556-1376
www.daap.uc.edu

ISBN #978-1-4951-4088-4

SPECIAL THANKS TO

Conservation and object preparation
Ashleigh Schieszer, Holly Prochaska, and Staff
The Preservation Services and Lab
A collaborative lab between the University of Cincinnati and the Library of
Cincinnati and Hamilton County

Digitization
Eira Tansey (archivist) and Nathan Tallman
(content strategist)
Archives & Rare Books Library

Sara Woolf
School of Planning

Research
Sara Woolf and Mark Carper
School of Planning

Translation
Elad Mokadi
School of Planning

Metadata
Carolyn Hansen
Archives & Rare Book Library

Collection Archived by
Kevin Grace
Archives & Rare Book Library

Reference/Collections
Suzanne Maggard Reller
Archives & Rare Book Library

Gallery Supervision
Aaron J. Cowan
DAAP Galleries

IN THE PUBLIC INTEREST:

The Life and Work of

Regional Planning Pioneer

Ladislas Segoe

(1894–1983)

February 15–April 5, 2015
Philip M. Meyers, Jr. Memorial Gallery
College of Design, Architecture, Art and Planning
University of Cincinnati

October 25–November 22, 2015
Bibliowicz Family Gallery and Garden
Milstein Hall
College of Art, Architecture and Planning
Cornell University

March 23–May 22, 2016
P. K. Huenich Gallery for Experimental Art and Architecture
(PeKA Gallery)
Segoe Building/Amado Building
Faculty of Architecture and Town Planning
Technion City
Technion—Israel Institute of Technology

LADISLAS SEGOE & ASSOCIATES
• CITY PLANNERS
• CONSULTING ENGINEERS

LADISLAS SEGOE

GWYNNE BUILDING • MAIN STREET AT SIXTH
CINCINNATI 2, OHIO TELEPHONE 721-6255

חייו ועבודתו של חלוץ בתכנון אזורי

לדיסלב סֶגו

(1894–1983)

15 בפברואר   5 באפריל 2015
Philip M. Meyers, Jr. Memorial Gallery
College of Design, Architecture, Art and Planning
University of Cincinnati

25 באוקטובר   22 בנובמבר 2015
Bibliowicz Family Gallery and Garden
Milstein Hall
College of Art, Architecture and Planning
Cornell University

23 במרץ   22 במאי 2016
הגלריה לארכיטקטורה ולאמנות ניסויית בטכניון ע"ש פ.ק. הניך
בניין אמאדו/ סגו
הפקולטה לארכיטקטורה ובינוי ערים
הטכניון מכון טכנולוגי לישראל

הוצאה מיוחדת לרגל התערוכה

בסיועה הנדיב של
Ladislas and Vilma Segoe Family Foundation

00.001
Ladislas Segoe Sitting at Desk
Black and white photographic print
mounted on paper
Imogen Cunningham
c.1947

TABLE OF CONTENTS

In his long and distinguished career, Segoe:

Prepared the first comprehensive plan for a major American city—Cincinnati, OH—in 1925, which included Northern Kentucky and was a forerunner of regional planning;

━━━━━━━━━━━━━━━

Along with Alfred Bettman and John Blandford of the Bureau of Government Research, prepared the first municipal capital budget in the United States;

━━━━━━━━━━━━━━━

Wrote with Bettman in 1928 the Standard City Planning Enabling Act;

━━━━━━━━━━━━━━━

In 1931, first used the concept of an urban growth boundary for Lexington, KY to control urban physical expansion. He thereby foresaw urban sprawl and paved the way for the most famous application of the growth boundary in Portland, OR more than a half century later;

Headed the research staff that wrote in 1937 *Our Cities: Their Role in the National Economy*, a landmark report of the Urbanism Committee of the National Resources Committee and the first federal comprehensive study of the nation's urban problems;

━━━━━━━━━━━━━━━

Wrote in 1941 for ICMA, *Local Planning Administration*, later called *Principles and Practice of Urban Planning* and now updated as *Local Planning: Contemporary Principles and Practice*. Dennis O'Darrow has called it a "godsend" and "... undoubtedly the most influential planning book in the United States during the first half of the 20th century."[1]

FOREWORD

On behalf of our College of Design Architecture, Art and Planning (DAAP), I would like to express my gratitude to the Ladislas and Vilma Segoe Family Foundation and its trustees, Lewis G. Gatch and David W. Ellison III. They have provided generous support to bring the Segoe Collections of the University of Cincinnati and Cornell University Libraries together for an exhibition of his career at both institutions and at the foundation-funded Segoe Building of the Technion-Israel Institute of Technology. This travelling exhibition is a collaboration of three of the world's premier institutions in their fields: DAAP, the College of Art, Architecture and Planning at Cornell, and the Faculty of Architecture and Town Planning at the Technion, as well as three world class university libraries. The enterprise enriches our understanding of the history of planning in the United States and its origins in Europe, and it demonstrates once again the global reach of exceptional, visionary individuals such as Ladislas Segoe.

Robert Probst
Dean, College of Design, Architecture, Art, and Planning
University of Cincinnati

THE AMERICAN INSTITUTE OF CERTIFIED PLANNERS

Designates

LADISLAS SEGOE, AICP

a

PLANNING PIONEER

Nationally renown planning consultant; co-inventor of the comprehensive plan; edited Local Planning Administration, "the most influential planning book in the U.S. during the first half of the twentieth century."

March 25, 1991

Sumner M. Sharpe
President

Israel Stollman
Executive Director

00.003
Award from American Institute
of Certified Planners Designating
Ladislas Segoe, a Planning Pioneer
Ivory paper mounted on wood;
acrylic overlay
American Institute of Certified Planners
1991

The Emergence of the Professional Planning Consultant

From 1921 through 1968, the career of Cincinnati-based Ladislas Segoe (1894–1983) paralleled the evolution of planning. Frequently instrumental in the development and perfection of American planning practice, he was involved in all levels and nearly all fields of planning. Through his widespread and successful consulting work, his publishing and his speaking, Segoe was a tireless advocate of independent, professional planning. Despite the Depression, World War II, the problems of urban renewal in the 1950s and civic unrest in the 1960s, he maintained a successful planning practice. That success was due to the strength of his personality, the coherence of his vision of planning as an encompassing process, his conscientious follow-through, and his insistence that planners be responsible, reasonable and honest professionals. He was one of the earliest city planning consultants in the US, advocated throughout his career for the increased presence of private planning firms and is one of only 83 individuals who has been named a "National Planning Pioneer" by the American Planning Association.[2, 3]

01

The European Years
1894–1921

01.009
Ladislas Segoe as a Young Boy
Black and white photographic print;
mounted on paper
Berky Deszo
1899

The European Years
1894–1921

Ladislas Segoe, "Laci" to his friends, was born to a Jewish family in Debrecen, Hungary on August 17, 1894. Mobilized while still a student, he entered the military and served for three and a half years as an ordinance officer, or more specifically, a mounted artillery officer, in World War I. Following the completion of his university studies in Budapest in 1919, he was awarded a Diploma in Civil Engineering. However, he was more than technically capable and was an intellectual in every sense.

"THE PLANNERS WHO CAME AFTER HIM WERE LIKE PYGMIES FOLLOWING A GIANT." [4]

Jack Benjamin, friend and lawyer

He was fluent in French and German, as well as English and his native Hungarian, and favored tailor made suits. Vilma Czittler, a young soprano whom he met in Budapest, was fun-loving and creative and brought out that side of his character.[4] Throughout their lives, they traveled frequently. Perhaps their upper middle class, middle European education and well to do family backgrounds attracted them to each other. In addition, his membership in the Austro-Hungarian officer corps accounted for his elitist and arrogant streak, and his requirement for perfection in his work. He never lost his accent and always dressed in the tie and jacket that were customary for his class and time in Europe.[2, 3]

01.020
Ladislas Segoe's Engineering Degree
Paper
Budapest University of Technology
and Economics
1919

01.008
Ladislas Segoe Doing Handstand
Black and white photographic print
Photographer unknown
c.1910s

01.003
Manuscript Map of Budapest
Tracing paper; graphite and blue ink
Ladislas Segoe
c.1910s

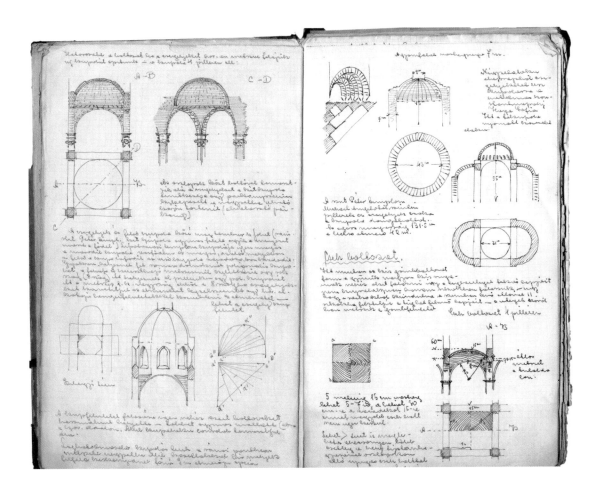

01.019
Manuscript Notes and Drawings
Paper; blue-gray cover boards;
bound with brown cotton twill tape
Ladislas Segoe
c.1910s

Segoe

1918.

BAND VIII.   HEFT 3.

STÄDTEBAULICHE VORTRÄGE

AUS DEM

SEMINAR FÜR STÄDTEBAU
AN DER KÖNIGLICHEN TECHNISCHEN HOCHSCHULE ZU BERLIN

HERAUSGEGEBEN

VON

DEN LEITERN DES SEMINARS FÜR STÄDTEBAU

JOSEPH BRIX   UND   **FELIX GENZMER**

STADTBAURAT A. D.   KGL. GEHEIMER HOFBAURAT
GEHEIMER REGIERUNGSRAT   ETATSM. PROFESSOR AN DER KGL. TECHN. HOCHSCHULE
ETATSM. PROFESSOR AN DER KGL. TECHN. HOCHSCHULE   ZU BERLIN
ZU BERLIN

AUS DEM VII. UND VIII. VORTRAGSZYKLUS

VOM FRANZÖSISCHEN STÄDTEBAU ZWEITER TEIL

VON Dr.-Ing. J. STÜBBEN, GEHEIMER OBERBAURAT, BERLIN-GRUNEWALD

MIT 90 IN DEN TEXT EINGEDRUCKTEN ABBILDUNGEN

BERLIN 1915
VERLAG VON WILHELM ERNST & SOHN.

01.018
Stadtebauliche Vortrage Band VIII. Heft 3.
Urban Lectures in the Department of
Urban Design at the Royal Institute
of Technology in Berlin
Paper
Verlag Von Wilhelm Ernst & Sohn
1915

University lectures retained by Segoe from when he was
a student.

585.

Konyhakocsik.

01.021b
Book of Postcards Showing Military Life
During World War I
Black and white photographic prints; paper
cover boards; bound with white cotton string
Creator unknown
c.1915

Segoe served in the Austrian-Hungarian army in WWI.
Includes 30 photographic postcards which seem to
document military life (perhaps Segoe's unit?). Back
of postcards have printed or manuscript information
in Hungarian.

01.005

Budapest: Twelve Little Photography

Twelve black and white photographic prints

bound in accordion style

Divald Grafikai Muintezet

c.1920s

Photographs of structures in Budapest of cultural and historical significance including: Parlement; Castle Vajdahunyad; Elisabeth Bridge; The Opera; Bridge of Francis Joseph; View from the Royal Castle; Royal Castle; Townpark with the Millenium-Monument; Fisher's Bastion with the Mathias Church; View from the St. Gerard hill; Bridge of chaines; The Royal Castle from the Mount of Gellert.

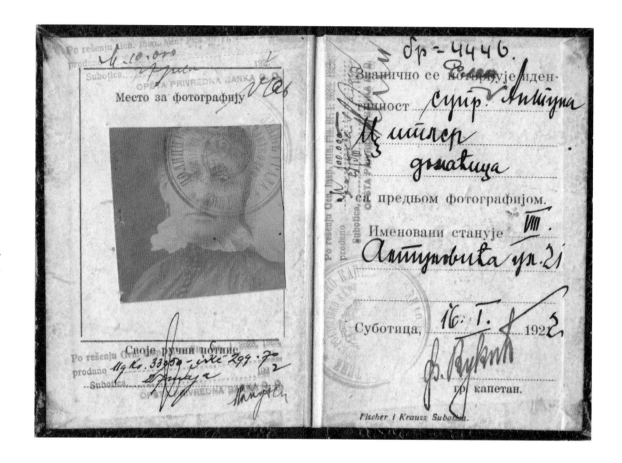

01.007
Vilma Segoe's Identification Card
Paper mounted on black book board; black
and white photographic print mounted on
paper; printed and manuscript text; stamped
Unknown creator
1921

01.010
Vilma Segoe in Pearls and Costume
Black and white photographic print; mounted
on paper
Unknown photographer
c.1921

01.011
Vilma Segoe Wearing Fur
and Holding Dog
Black and white photographic print
Unknown photographer
c.1920s

01.012
Vilma Segoe in Satin Costume
Black and white photographic print
Unknown photographer
c.1921

01.013
Vilma Segoe in Naval Costume
Black and white photographic print
Unknown photographer
c.1921

01.015
Vilma Segoe Posing Against Wall
Black and white photographic print;
mounted on board
Unknown photographer
c.1921

A)

B)

D)

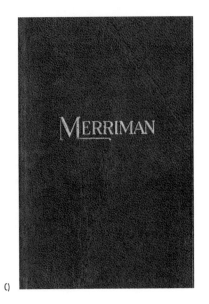

C)

A few of the many university texts that Segoe retained from his time as a student.

clockwise

A) **01.016**
Die deutsche Städt und ihre Verwaltung:
eine Einführung in die Kommunalpolitik
der Gegenwart
Monograph: paper
Otto Most
1913

B) **01.004**
Taschenbuch für Bauingenieure
Monograph: paper
Max Foerster
1914

C) **01.002**
Die Städtebau nach seinen künstlerischen
Grundsätzen: ein Beitrag zur Lösung
Moderner Fragen der Architektur und
Monumentalen Plastik unter Besonderer
Beziehung auf Wien
Monograph: Paper
Camillo Sitte
1922

D) **01.017**
American Civil Engineers' Handbook
Monograph: paper; leather bound
Merriman Mansfield
1920

01.001c + d
Manuscript Book of Poems
Paper and blue ink; bound in purple cloth
covers; craft paper book cover
Ladislas Segoe
c.1910s

The young engineer as a poet.

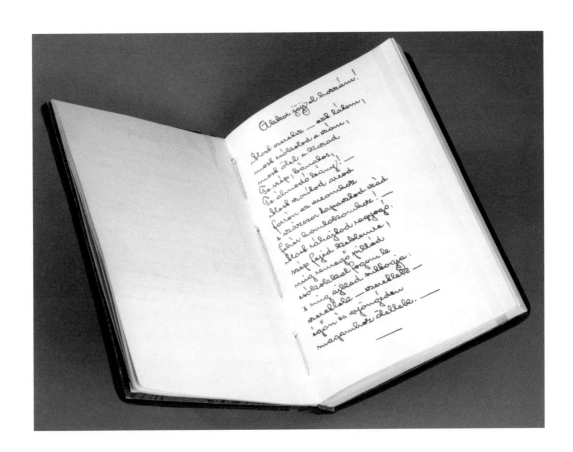

02

Immigration and Early Practice
1921–1929

02.003
Ladlslas Segoe Standing in Front of Trees
Black and white photographic print
Unknown photographer
c.1920s

Immigration and Early Practice
1921–1929

Uncomfortable with the Communist regime in Hungary following the First World War, at the invitation of a relative, he immigrated to the United States. Segoe quickly found employment with a consulting group, the Technical Advisory Corporation (TAC), which had only recently entered the area of planning consultation. It was as an employee of TAC that Segoe came to Cincinnati for the first time. His assignment was to direct the technical work on projects in Dayton and Cincinnati. This work yielded the Official City Plan of Cincinnati, Ohio (1925), the first comprehensive plan for a major city in the United States, as well as a similar plan for Dayton (1926). A Cincinnati Newspaper noted that, "...Segoe is a thorough student of economic, social, and industrial situations and backgrounds. He is intelligent, broadly trained, and imaginative. He is in no sense just a physical planner." After these projects, he already held outside contracts as an independent consultant.[2, 3] Working with the attorney Alfred Bettman, the chairman of Cincinnati's planning commission, who was Segoe's long term mentor, they developed the "Segoe-Bettman theory" of planning[6], which the American Institute of Certified Planners has cited as the theory of the comprehensive plan. While Bettman had a better sense of the political environment, Segoe had a better sense of planning as a process, so both individually and together, they made important contributions to the formulation of the Standard City Planning Enabling Act, published by the U.S. Department of Commerce in 1928.[3]

02.001

Ladislas Segoe's United States Passport
Paper mounted on book board; black and
white photographic print mounted on paper;
printed and manuscript text; stamped
United States State Department
1928

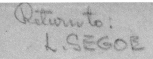

No. 665

IN THE

Supreme Court of the United States

OCTOBER TERM, 1925

THE VILLAGE OF EUCLID and HARRY W. STEIN,
Inspector of Buildings,

Appellants,

v.

THE AMBLER REALTY COMPANY,

Appellee.

Appeal from the District Court of the United States for the Northern District of Ohio, Eastern Division.

**MOTION FOR LEAVE TO FILE BRIEF, AMICI CURIAE
AND
BRIEF ON BEHALF OF THE NATIONAL CONFERENCE ON CITY PLANNING, THE NATIONAL HOUSING ASSOCIATION AND THE MASSACHUSETTS FEDERATION OF TOWN PLANNING BOARDS, AMICI CURIAE.**

ALFRED BETTMAN,

*Counsel for The National Conference on
City Planning, The Ohio State Con-
ference on City Planning, The Na-
tional Housing Association and The
Massachusetts Federation of Town
Planning Boards, Amici Curiae.*

02.007

In the Supreme Court of the United States,
October Term, 1925

Monograph: paper
James Metzenbaum
1925

The Euclid (Ohio) decision established zoning in
the United States. Segoe provided planning input
to Bettman's influential brief.

02.006
The Official City Plan of Cincinnati, Ohio
Monograph: Paper
Cincinnati City Planning Commission
1925

The first comprehensive plan for a major city in the United States.

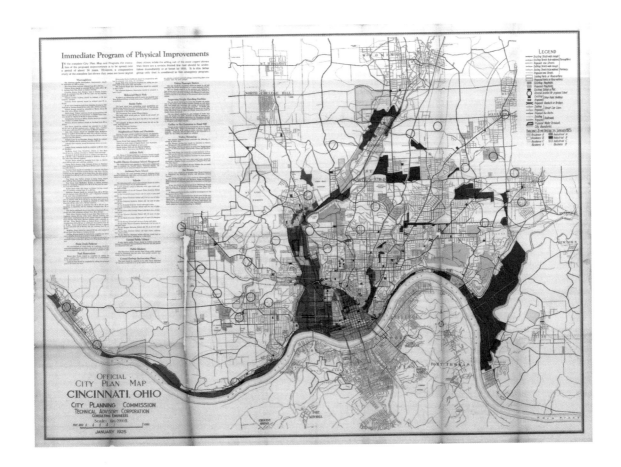

39

02.008
Official City Plan Map of Cincinnati, Ohio
Paper
City Planning Commission
1925

WHAT THE BONDS ARE FOR

and

WHY YOU
SHOULD VOTE FOR THEM

**Let's Keep on
IMPROVING
CINCINNATI**

The Proposed City Improvements for 1928 Will

ADD ONLY 5 CENTS

per $1,000 Valuation to Your 1928 Tax Bill

READ THIS PAMPHLET AND YOU WILL
UNDERSTAND WHY

Vote $\boxed{\text{X} \mid \text{YES}}$ On All the
Bond Issues.

BOND ISSUE COMMITTEE,
L. B. BLAKEMORE, Clerk of Council,
Secretary.

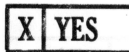 5

02.004
What the Bonds are for and Why You
Should Vote for Them
Pamphlet: paper
Cincinnati Bond Issue Committee
c.1928

Pamphlet explaining why voters should approve
authorization of city bonds for general city improvements
in Cincinnati. Includes financial breakdown of the
proposed funds.

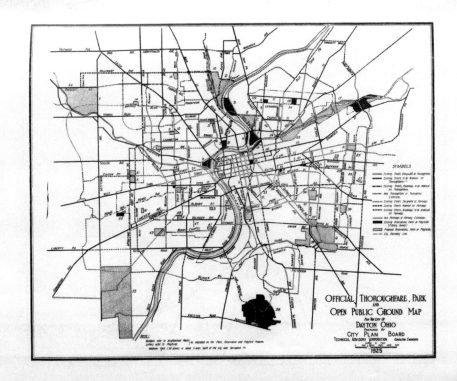

02.005c
A Comprehensive City Plan for Dayton,
Ohio: Chapters IV, V, VI and VII
Paper
Dayton City Plan Board
1926

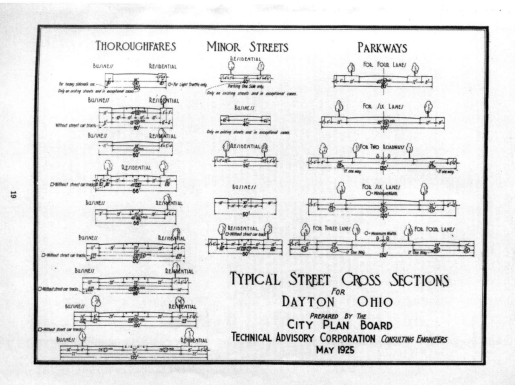

THOROUGHFARES · MINOR STREETS · PARKWAYS

TYPICAL STREET CROSS SECTIONS
FOR
DAYTON OHIO
PREPARED BY THE
CITY PLAN BOARD
TECHNICAL ADVISORY CORPORATION *Consulting Engineers*
MAY 1925

19

42

02.005b
A Comprehensive City Plan for Dayton,
Ohio: Chapters IV, V, VI and VII
Paper
Dayton City Plan Board
1926

02.003
Ladislas Segoe and Vilma Segoe
at the Beach
Black and white photographic print
Unknown photographer
c.1926

03

The Depression, Professional Practice and the Urbanism Study
1930–1939

03.002
Ladislas Segoe Wearing Suit
Black and white photographic print
Bachrach Studio
c.1930

The city plan for Lexington, Kentucky (1931) is evidence of the timelessness and longevity of Segoe's planning. The concept of a belt designating an urban service area is still used successfully in that city. By limiting the area available for urban services such as water supply and sewer lines, the government can keep growth in check. Furthermore, other metropolitan areas, most notably Portland, Oregon, have adopted this method to control suburban "sprawl" —a contemporary planning issue foreseen by Segoe. Segoe claimed, "...truly adequate planning for any metropolitan community must embrace not only the entire city but all of the outlying urban and urbanizing areas." He also directed the first federal study of urban problems in the United States, which was published in 1937 as *Our Cities and Their Role in the National Economy*. It stressed the need for a "sound long-term land policy," which could properly direct urban and economic development.[2, 3] What is remarkable about these achievements is that that took place after the cataclysmic stock market crash of 1929 and the resulting malaise of the Depression.

TRULY ADEQUATE PLANNING FOR ANY METROPOLITAN COMMUNITY MUST EMBRACE NOT ONLY THE ENTIRE CITY, BUT ALL OF THE OUTLYING URBAN AND URBANIZING AREAS.[4]

48

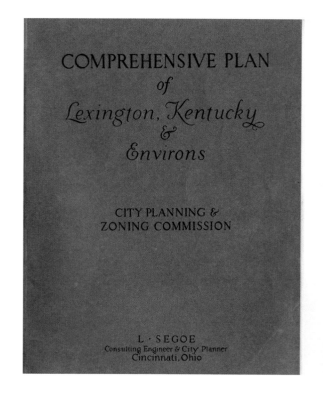

COMPREHENSIVE PLAN
of
Lexington, Kentucky
&
Environs

CITY PLANNING &
ZONING COMMISSION

L · SEGOE
Consulting Engineer & City Planner
Cincinnati, Ohio

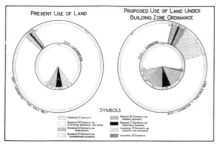

WELL DEVELOPED LOCAL BUSINESS DISTRICT
(Woodland and High Streets)

03.004a + b
Comprehensive Plan for Lexington
and its Environs
Monograph: paper
Ladislas Segoe
1931

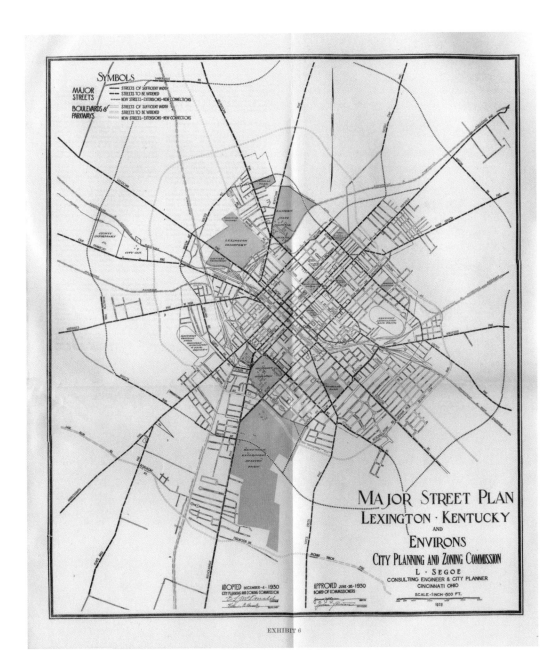

EXHIBIT 6

03.004c

Comprehensive Plan for Lexington
and its Environs
Paper
Ladislas Segoe
1931

03.001
Ladislas Segoe with Tennis Racquet
Black and white photographic print
Unknown photographer
c.1930s

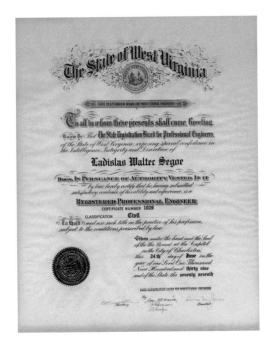

03.003
Ohio Professional Engineer Certificate for
Ladislas Segoe
Paper
Ohio State Board of Registration for
Professional Engineers and Surveyors
1935

03.008
West Virginia Professional Engineer
Certificate for Ladislas Segoe
Paper
West Virginia State Registration Board
for Professional Engineers
1939

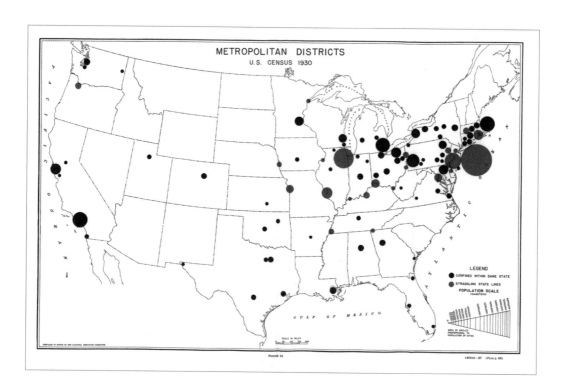

03.010b

Map From Our cities: Their Role
in the National Economy
Paper
Urbanism Committee
1937

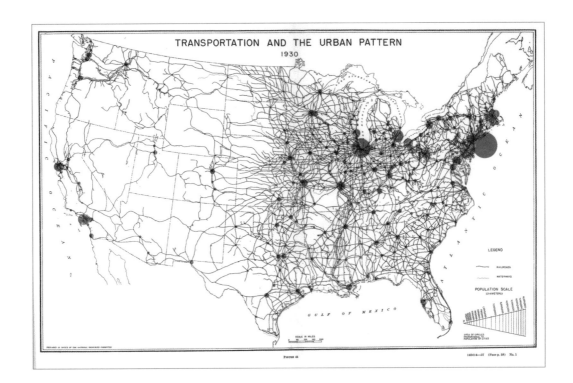

03.010c

Map From Our cities: Their Role
in the National Economy
Paper
Urbanism Committee
1937

04

The Second World War, the "Green Bible,"
and Planning the Big Cities
1940–1959

04.010
Ladislas Segoe Wearing Suit and Tie Clip
Black and white photographic print
Unknown photographer
c.1940

The Second World War, the "Green Bible," and Planning the Big Cities
1940–1959

Depression era attempts to integrate programs of industrial recovery into comprehensive planning were now shifted toward integrating wartime defense programs into planning. They were also shifted toward adjusting patterns of municipal finance to secure both victory, on the international level, and fiscal responsibility, at the local level. During this period, Segoe prepared comprehensive plans for a number of major cities, including San Francisco, Cincinnati, Richmond and Detroit.

In Detroit, Segoe had to convert his conception of "City in a region" into "regional planning for a metropolitan area" due to the effects of World War II. Southeastern Michigan had become both a diversely urbanized and diversely industrialized region. Thus, planning for Detroit needed to acknowledge not only its immediate "hinterland" as a metropolitan area, but also its embeddedness in an industrialized region. His policies and procedures accomplishing this established a model for the professional.[3]

Also at this time, at the behest of the International City Managers Association (ICMA), he compiled and edited the first edition of *Local Planning Administration*, (1941). This book, the "Green Bible," is the work that is for many most associated with his name, and it made him known to all students and practitioners of planning. The book has been widely used, not only in virtually all schools of planning, but by local government administrators in all parts of the United States, and in many other countries as well, as a continuing guide to the complex problems of urban development.[3] Its comprehensiveness and usefulness, as well as its traditional green cover, have led to its nickname. This book, one of the most important planning books of the twentieth century, remains a recognized basic planning text and is still in widespread use nationwide.

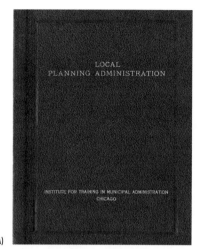

A)

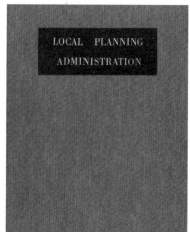

B)

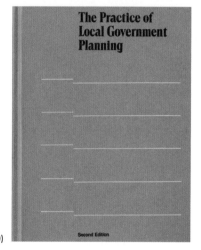

D)

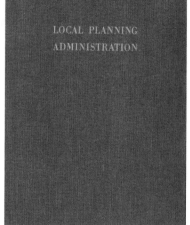

C)

clockwise

A) **04.009a**
Local Planning Administration
("The Green Bible" 1st edition)
Monograph: paper; bound in book board
Ladislas Segoe
1941

B) **04.008**
Local Planning Administration
("The Green Bible" 2nd edition)
Paper
Ladislas Segoe
1948

C) **04.007**
Local Planning Administration
("The Green Bible" 3rd edition)
Monograph: paper; bound in book board
Mary McLean (editor)
1959

D) **04.002**
The Practice of Local Government Planning
("The Green Bible" 4th edition)
Monograph: paper; bound in book board
Frank S. So and Judith Getzels
1988

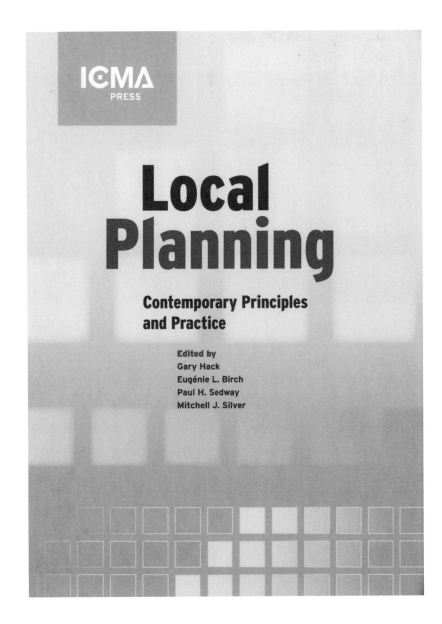

04.001a
Local Planning: Contemporary Principles
and Practice
("The Green Bible" 5th edition)
Monograph: paper; bound in book board
Gary Hack
2009

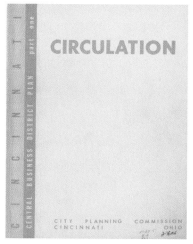

A)

B)

D)

C)

clockwise

A) **04.003**
MasterPlan, Chillicothe, Ohio, and Environs
Monograph: paper
Ladislas Segoe
1949

B) **04.006**
Circulation, Part One of the Cincinnati Central Business District Plan
Monograph: paper
Cincinnati City Planning Commission
1958

C) **04.004**
Basic Features of Comprehensive Master Plan for Ashland Kentucky and Environs
Monograph: paper; spiral bound
Ladislas Segoe and Associates
1959

D) **04.005**
Comprehensive Master Plan, Bellaire, Ohio: Proposed Subdivision Regulations
Monograph: paper; spiral bound
Bellaire City Planning Commission
1963

CITY and REGIONAL PLANNING PAPERS

BY ALFRED BETTMAN

EDITED BY ARTHUR C. COMEY

HARVARD CITY PLANNING STUDIES NO. 13

Blackstone Studios

ALFRED BETTMAN
1873–1945

04.014a + b
City and Regional Planning Papers
Monograph: paper
Alfred Bettman
1946

Attorney Alfred Bettman, the chairman of Cincinnati's planning commission, was Segoe's long term mentor. Together they developed the "Segoe-Bettman theory" of planning[6], which the American Institute of Certified Planners has cited as the theory of the comprehensive plan.

04.016b + c
Downtown Riverfront Redevelopment
Plan; Metropolitan Master Plan
Paper; spiral bound
Cincinnati City Planning Commission
1946

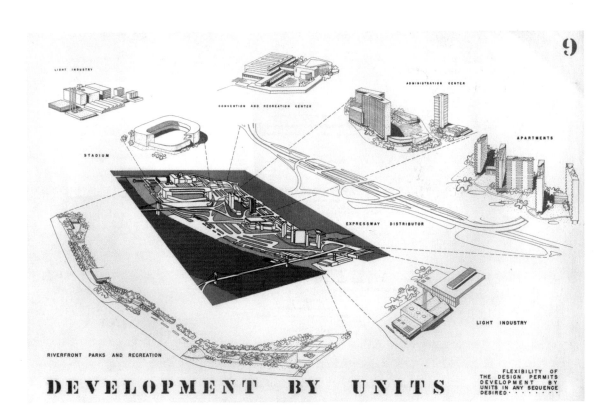

9

LIGHT INDUSTRY

CONVENTION AND RECREATION CENTER

ADMINISTRATION CENTER

APARTMENTS

STADIUM

EXPRESSWAY DISTRIBUTOR

LIGHT INDUSTRY

RIVERFRONT PARKS AND RECREATION

FLEXIBILITY OF
THE DESIGN PERMITS
DEVELOPMENT BY
UNITS IN ANY SEQUENCE
DESIRED · · · · · · ·

DEVELOPMENT BY UNITS

next spread

04.027a + d
The Plan for Downtown Cincinnati:
Report on the Plan for the Central
Business District
Paper
Hammer and Company Associates; Alan M.
Voorhees & Associates; Rogers, Taliaferro,
Kostritsky, Lamb.
1964

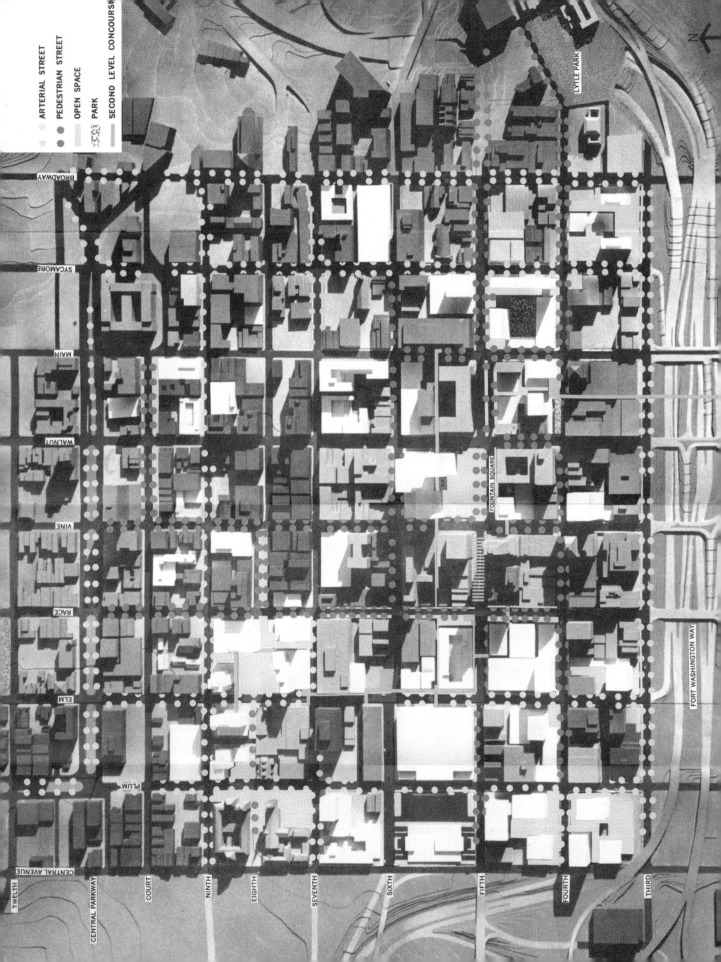

ARTERIAL STREET
PEDESTRIAN STREET
OPEN SPACE
PARK
SECOND LEVEL CONCOURSE

BROADWAY
SYCAMORE
MAIN
WALNUT
VINE
RACE
ELM
PLUM
CENTRAL AVENUE

TWELFTH
CENTRAL PARKWAY
COURT
NINTH
EIGHTH
SEVENTH
SIXTH
FIFTH
FOURTH
THIRD

LYTLE PARK

FOUNTAIN SQUARE

FORT WASHINGTON WAY

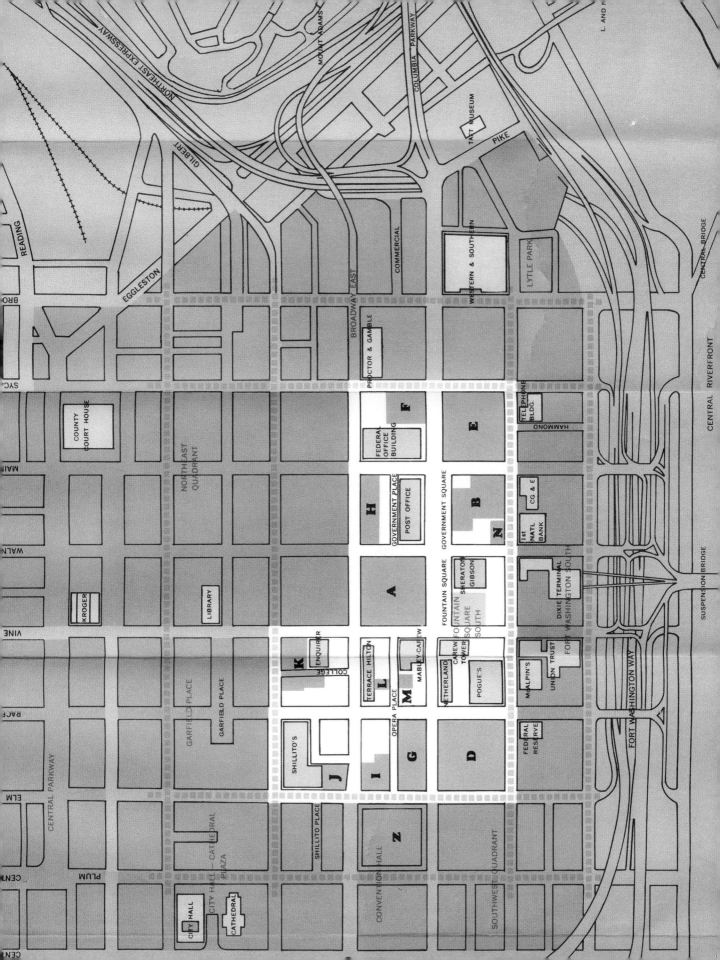

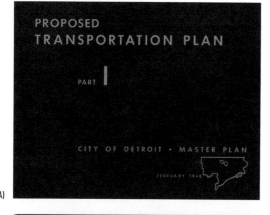

A)

B)

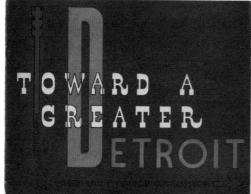

D)

PROPOSED GENERALIZED
LAND USE PLAN

CITY OF DETROIT · MASTER PLAN

MAY 1947

C)

clockwise

A) **04.011**
City of Detroit, A Master Plan Report.
No. 6, Proposed Transportation Plan. Part
1, Motor Freight Terminals, Port Facilities
Monograph: paper
Detroit City Plan Commission
1948

B) **04.012a**
City of Detroit, A Master Plan Report.
No. 7. Proposed Cultural Center Plan
Monograph: paper
Detroit City Plan Commission
April 1948

C) **04.028**
Master Plan of Detroit, Proposed
Generalized Land Use Plan
Monograph: paper; spiral bound
Detroit Metropolitan Area
Regional Planning Commission
1947

D) **04.033a**
Toward a Greater Detroit. Looking Ahead
with the City Plan Commission
Monograph: paper
Melvin Lubar; Detroit City Plan Commission
c.1944

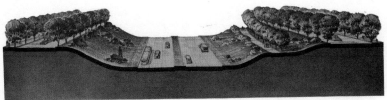

GRAND RIVER EXPRESSWAY FROM WEST CHICAGO DOWNTOWN WOULD CARRY BUSES FROM THE NORTHWEST. SLOPES WOULD BE LANDSCAPED BELOW SERVICE ROADS AND INCIDENTAL IMPROVEMENTS WOULD INCLUDE PATHS FOR PEDESTRIANS

GRAND RIVER EXPRESSWAY BEYOND WEST CHICAGO WOULD PROVIDE FOR RAPID TRANSIT CARS IN THE PLANTED DIVIDING MALL AND LOCAL BUSES WOULD USE SERVICE ROADS

JOHN C. LODGE EXPRESSWAY WOULD INCLUDE A PROMENADE IN THE LANDSCAPED RIGHT-OF-WAY. PAVED SHOULDERS FOR DISABLED VEHICLES WOULD BE AN IMPORTANT SAFETY FEATURE OF THIS EXPRESSWAY AND ALL OTHERS

HASTINGS EXPRESSWAY WOULD CARRY EXPRESS BUSES TO THE CENTRAL BUSINESS DISTRICT SOUTH OF THE CROSSTOWN. BOTH WALKS AND BICYCLE PATHS WOULD BE INCLUDED IN THE INCIDENTAL IMPROVEMENTS

04.025b
Detroit Expressway and Transit System
Paper
W. Earle Andrews
1945

04.030a–f
Detroit Maps From 1799–1957
35mm color slide
Unknown creator
c. 20th-c.

Historical maps showing land planning for Detroit.
Complete set (9) includes: Detroit 1799; The governor
and judges plan: Detroit 1807; Detroit 1820; Detroit
1870; Regional land use plan: Detroit area; Generalized
land use: Detroit area; Detroit 1942; Detroit 1920;
Detroit 1890.

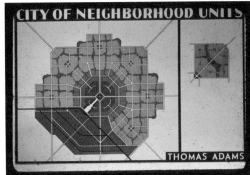

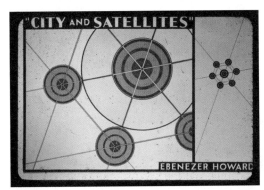

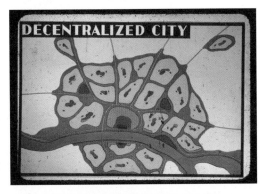

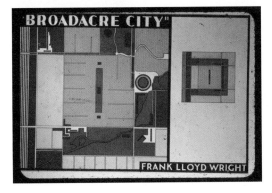

04.031a,b,d,e,h,j
Conceptual View of Detroit
35mm color slide
Unknown creator
c.20th-c.

10 slides in the complete set; Includes: The regional city/ Clarence Stein; City of Neighborhood Units/Thomas Adams; City patterns: legend; City and satellites/Ebenezer Howard; Decentralized city (subcommunities); City in the landscape/L.K. (Ludwig Karl) Hilberseimer; A radical city/ Paul Wolf; Broadacre city/Frank L. Wright; A linear city: Russian scheme; Contemporary city/Le Corbusier.

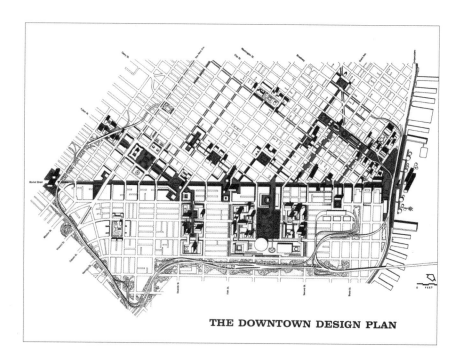

THE DOWNTOWN DESIGN PLAN

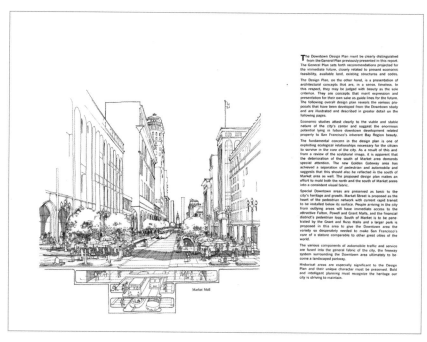

Market Mall

The Downtown Design Plan must be clearly distinguished from the General Plan previously presented in this report. The General Plan sets forth recommendations projected for the immediate future, closely related to present economic feasibility, available land, existing structures and codes.

The Design Plan, on the other hand, is a presentation of architectural concepts that are, in a sense, timeless. In this respect, they may be judged with beauty as the sole criterion. They are concepts that merit expression and presentation for their own sake as guide lines for the future. The following overall design plan reveals the various proposals that have been developed from the Downtown study and are illustrated and described in greater detail on the following pages.

Economic studies attest clearly to the viable and stable nature of the city's center and suggest the enormous potential lying in future downtown development related properly to San Francisco's inherent Bay Region beauty.

The fundamental concern in the design plan is one of exploiting ecological relationships necessary for the citizen to survive in the core of the city. As a result of this and from a review of the sculptural image, it is apparent that the deterioration of the south of Market area demands special attention. The new Golden Gateway area has achieved a separation of pedestrian and automobile and suggests that this should also be reflected in the south of Market area as well. The proposed design plan makes an effort to mold both the north and the south of Market areas into a consistent visual fabric.

Special Downtown areas are preserved as basic to the city's heritage and growth. Market Street is proposed as the heart of the pedestrian network with current rapid transit to be installed below its surface. People arriving in city from outlying areas will have immediate access to the attractive Fulton, Powell and Grant Malls, and the financial district's pedestrian loop. South of Market is to be penetrated by the Grant and Russ Malls and a larger park is proposed in this area to give the Downtown area the variety so desperately needed to make San Francisco's core of a stature comparable to other great cities of the world.

The various components of automobile traffic and service are fused into the general fabric of the city, the freeway system surrounding the Downtown area ultimately to become a landscaped parkway.

Historical areas are especially significant to the Design Plan and their unique character must be preserved. Bold and intelligent planning must recognize the heritage our city is striving to maintain.

70

04.038d + e
Downtown San Francisco
Monograph: paper; spiral bound
San Francisco Department of City Planning
c.1950s

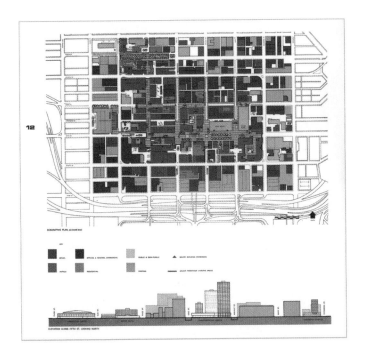

04.045b + c
A Revitalization Plan for the City Core of
Cincinnati, Ohio
Monograph: paper; spiral bound
Victor Gruen Associates; Larry Smith and
Company
1962

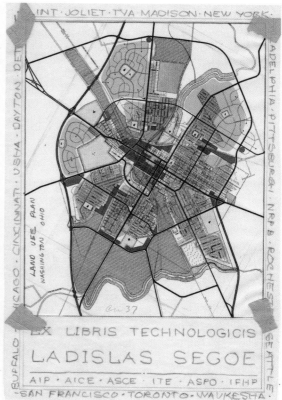

05.026a–05.026c

Manuscript Notes and Draft of Ladislas
Segoe's Professional Bookplate

Paper; color ink; graphite; red color pencil;
masking tape

Ladislas Segoe

c.1960s

Handmade maquette for Segoe's professional bookplate
includes handwritten notes and directions for printer.

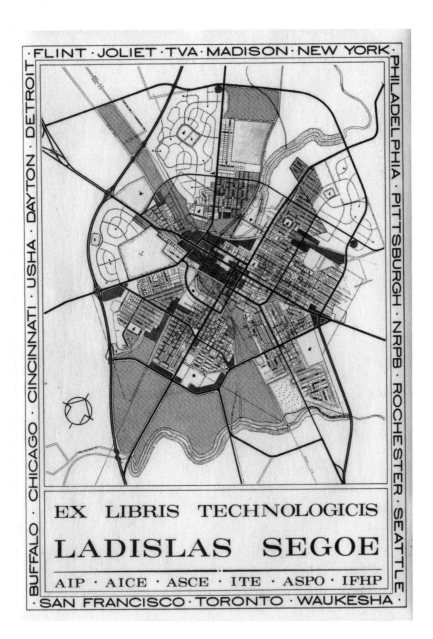

FLINT · JOLIET · TVA · MADISON · NEW YORK
DETROIT · DAYTON · USHA · CINCINNATI · CHICAGO · BUFFALO
PHILADELPHIA · PITTSBURGH · NRPB · ROCHESTER · SEATTLE

EX LIBRIS TECHNOLOGICIS

LADISLAS SEGOE

AIP · AICE · ASCE · ITE · ASPO · IFHP

SAN FRANCISCO · TORONTO · WAUKESHA

05.004
Ladislas Segoe's Professional Bookplate
Paper
Ladislas Segoe
c.1960s

04.042b
Ladislas Segoe's Rolodex
Metal Rolodex file: paper; plastic tabs
Ladislas Segoe
c.1950s

04.041c
Zoning Cases Card File
Cardboard; paper; plastic tabs;
metal box pull
Ladislas Segoe
c.1950s

05

05.002
Photograph of Ladislas and Vilma Segoe
Sitting Near Pillar
Black and white photographic print
Photographer unknown
c.1960

Interstate Highways, Urban Redevelopment and Citizen Participation
1960–1968

The closing decade of Segoe's professional practice reveals a decided shift toward county and smaller city planning, done more often by his associates. Of these plans, many were integrated into the larger county context, demonstrating Segoe's concern for efficient urban development within a regional context. Also during this period, three subjects were of increasing concern to him: the planning implications of the much expanded interstate highway system, urban renewal, and citizen participation. Segoe sought to make the transportation systems responsive to proper land use patterns.[3] The new federal highway system had begun to alter radically accessibility functions not only among regions, but also within metropolitan areas.[3] His concerns anticipated urban sprawl. He also believed one of the responsibilities of the professional planner was to justify the plan to the community, so that in winning their consensus, citizen participation could be easily directed toward nonpartisan political support for the legislative adoption of the plan.[3] In the 60s as well, Segoe turned his attention to the education of planners and established a lecture series in city planning at the University of Cincinnati, financed by the Alfred Bettman Foundation. It is not clear what force these lectures had in curriculum development at the University of Cincinnati, but by 1963 both undergraduate and graduate planning programs had been established.[2] Increasingly in this time of their lives, Ladislas and Vilma mixed his professional practice with their leisure by traveling the world.

"LADISLAS DIDN'T COME CHEAP....HE SCRIBBLED FOR ABOUT 35–40 MINUTES AND HANDED ME A SINGLE SHEET OF PAPER. HE BILLED ME $3,500.... BUT I'LL TELL YOU, IT WAS WORTH EVERY DOLLAR...I THINK IT WAS HIS VERSATILITY THAT MADE HIM CLOSE TO BEING A GENIUS."[4]

Jack Benjamin, friend and lawyer

A)

B)

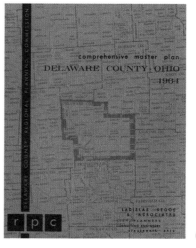

C)

D)

clockwise

A) **05.015**
Comprehensive Master Plan
of Flint, Michigan
Monograph: paper; spiral bound
Ladislas Segoe and Associates
1960

B) **05.018a**
Comprehensive Master Plan,
Coshocton, Ohio
Monograph: paper; spiral bound
Ladislas Segoe and Associates
1961

C) **05.008**
Comprehensive Master Plan,
Delaware County, Ohio
Monograph: paper; spiral bound
Ladislas Segoe and Associates
1964

D) **05.020**
Revised Elements, Comprehensive Plan,
Charleston, West Virginia.
Volume 1, Basic studies
Monograph: paper; spiral bound
Ladislas Segoe and Associates
1962

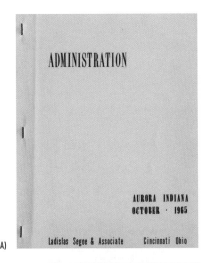

A)

B)

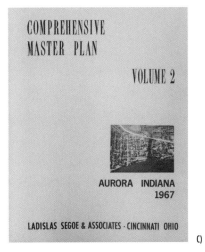

D)

C)

clockwise

A) **05.017**
Comprehensive Master Plan,
Aurora, Indiana: Administration
Monograph: paper
Ladislas Segoe and Associates
1965

B) **05.009**
Comprehensive Master Plan,
Cahokia, Illinois
Monograph: paper; spiral bound
Ladislas Segoe and Associates
1966

C/D) **05.016a–05.016b**
Comprehensive Master Plan,
Aurora, Indiana
Monograph: paper; spiral bound
Ladislas Segoe and Associates
1967

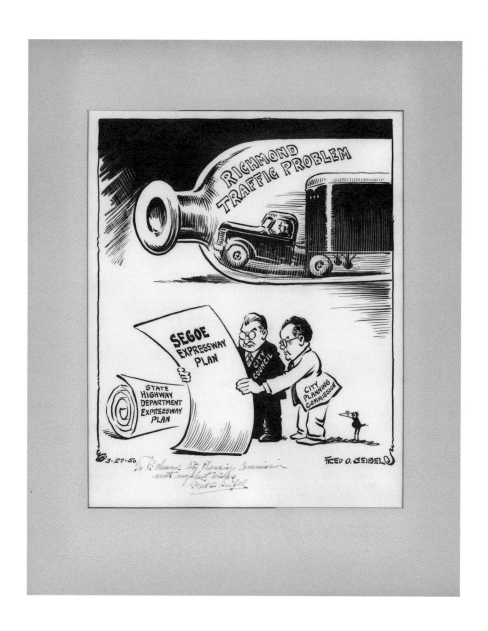

04.026
Richmond Traffic Problem Cartoon
Paper; illustration board
Fred O. Seibel
1950

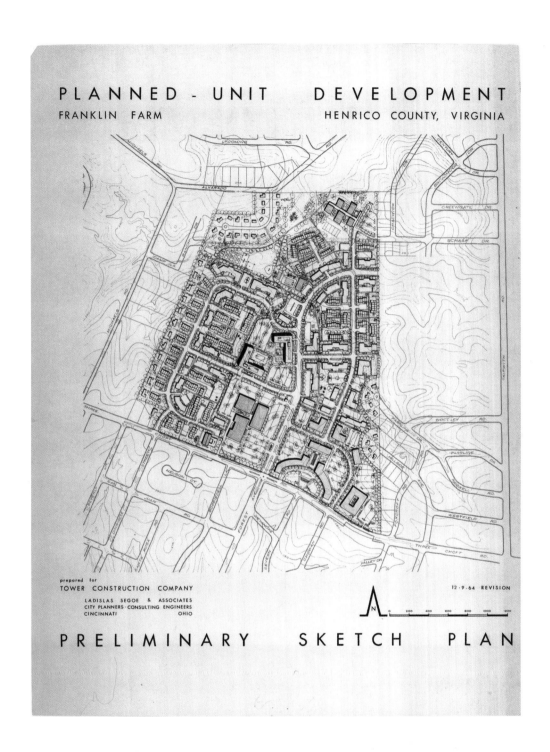

PLANNED - UNIT DEVELOPMENT

FRANKLIN FARM   HENRICO COUNTY, VIRGINIA

prepared for
TOWER CONSTRUCTION COMPANY

LADISLAS SEGOE & ASSOCIATES
CITY PLANNERS · CONSULTING ENGINEERS
CINCINNATI   OHIO

12·9·64 REVISION

PRELIMINARY SKETCH PLAN

05.014
Planned Unit Development Preliminary
Sketch Plan: Henrico County, Virginia
Monograph: paper
Ladislas Segoe and Associates
1964

84

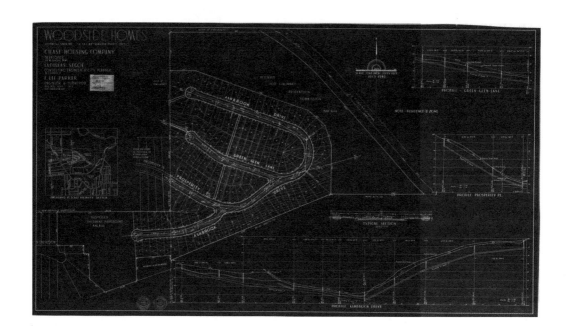

04.044e
Woodside Development
Blueprint
Ladislas Segoe
1940

B)

D)

04.044b + d
Woodside Development
Black and white photographic print (b);
color photograph (d.)
Creator unknown (b); Jennifer Latessa (d)
1940 (b); 2014 (d)

ADDRESSES
by
L. Segoe

File
No.

CITY PLANS

1	Short Bibliography on City Planning & Housing	
1	Intro. for Panel on Metropolitan & City-County Plans-APCA Conf., New Orleans	1953
1	"How to Prepare a General City Plan" - Ohio Planning Conference	1950
1	"Growth & Coordination of Metropolitan Areas,"-34th Anniv. Meet.-OPC, Dayton	1956
1	"Forecasts that are Shaping Cities Today," Urban Design Conf.Panel, Harvard	1956
1	Brief Discussion of Fundamentals, City Planning	1939
9	"Future of Metro. Cincinnati," Good Government League of Hamilton County	1955
13	Speech, etc.-Organization of Metrolitan Area in Sub-Communities, Buffalo.	
14	"Building Better Neighborhoods & Communities," Nat'l Comm.on Housing,Chicago	1946
18	"How Can Overall Community Planning be Done?"-Radio Address,Columbus Town Meet.	1947
20	"What Is This Job of Community Planning?"-Local Planning Institute, Detroit	1946
26	City Planning - Addresses - Madison, Wisconsin	1939
29	"How to Prepare a General City Plan," Ohio Planning Conference	1950
33	Why a City Plan - What is City Plan - What City Planning Can & Should Do for Your City.	
39	What City Planning Can do for your City.	
39	City Planning - Brief Discussion of Fundamentals (pp8, W. Va. Engineer)	1939
39	Community Planning - Brief Discussion of Fundamentals	
39	Comprehensive Plan for Lexington, Ky.	
39	City Planning In Kentucky	1933
39	What the City Plan Aims to do.	
39	City Planning - Rotary Club, Madison, Wisc.	1937
39	Major Factors effecting Future of American Cities	1934
39	"City & Reg. Planning & its Possibilities" - Woman's City Club, Cincinnati	1932
43	Municipal Planning in U.S.-2nd Inter-American Cong.of Municipalities,San.de.Chile	1941
46	City Planning & the Urbanism Study - Conference on Planning, Richmond, Va.	1936
58	"The Changing Form of the American City"-Univ. of California, Berkeley	1963
66.	"Planning Metropolitan Cincinnati - Basic Policies" - Cincinnati ASPO	1947
1	Citizen Housing & Planning Council - Detroit Plan	1945

COUNTY PLANS

11	Intro. for Panel on Metropolitan & City-County Plans - APCA Conf., New Orleans	1953
7	"Harford County - What Kind of a Community Should it Be?"	
8	"A Program for Tri-County Planning," Akron, Ohio Tri-County Reg. Planning Comm.	1957
41	Notes on County Planning	1940
41	Regional Planning for Hamilton County - (Woman's City Club Bulletin)	1931
41	County Planning - 23rd National Conference on City Planning, Rochester	1931

CONSULTANCY

2	Planning Consultant Services - Notes for talk at ASPO Conference	1959

Files numbered 0 - 57 in "Addresses" file.
     "   "   58 - 62 in "General" file.
     "   "   63 - 66 in "A.S.P.O." file.

- 1 -

06.001a
Addresses by L. Segoe, 1931–1964
Paper; typescript
Ladislas Segoe
1931–1964

List of presentations given by Segoe between 1931–1964.
Lists file number; Title; Occasion; Place; Date. Organized
according to topic of presentation.

THE OHIO PLANNING CONFERENCE
prizes the contributions of
THE ALFRED BETTMAN FOUNDATION
to the quality of planning education in Ohio
and the nation in pursuance of its aim:

"To further the scientific
application of sound planning
in the public interest on all
levels of government, local, state
and federal . . . "

Presented at the 45th annual meeting, in Cincinnati, Ohio, March 19, 1963

05.032
Acknowledgement from the Ohio
Planning Conference Praising
the Contributions of the Alfred
Bettman Foundation
Paper; black, gold, and red ink; glass; wood
Ohio Planning Conference
1963

Ohio Planning Conference Award to the Alfred Bettman
Foundation of which Segoe was president.

05.025a-05.025z (26)
Postcards Depicting Various Cities
Paper
Creator unknown
c.1940–1970

The Segoes combined their love of travel and love of cities.

CONCLUSION

An Appreciation of Service

In the introduction to *The American Planner: Biographies and Recollections*, Donald Krueckeberg identifies Segoe as one of the "new professionals" in that first generation to make planning their primary career: "The product of that early era was a new profession devoted to the unified and comprehensive planning of cities and regions to satisfy human needs with both beauty and efficiency. Like the larger society from which it grew, the planning movement contained numerous differences of emphasis and contradictions. Yet this powerful idea has its basis in the faith that reason, honesty and technical skills could be combined to guide the growth of the nation's cities into the twentieth century and toward a better way of life".[5] It was widely recognized through numerous awards that Ladislas Segoe personified the profession of planning.

at left

06.002
Ladislas Segoe
Black and white photographic print
Photographer unknown
c.1970s

05.030

Gift Acknowledgement to Ladislas and
Vilma Segoe from Technion — Israel
Institute of Technology

Black lacquered wood; cast bronze;
engraved metal

Technion, Israel Institute of Technology

c.1960s

WITH GRATITUDE FROM

HADASSAH

Ladislas and Vilma Segoe

For a Founders Gift
Two-Bed Patients Room
In Memory of his Sister
Lily Szegö

Hadassah-Hebrew University Medical Center
Jerusalem, Israel

ONE OF THE TWELVE STAINED GLASS WINDOWS BY MARC CHAGALL WHICH CROWN THE SYNAGOGUE OF THE HADASSAH-HEBREW UNIVERSITY MEDICAL CENTER, JERUSALEM, ISRAEL

05.001
Gift Acknowledgement to Ladislas and
Vilma Segoe from Hadassah-Hebrew
University Medical Center
White paper portfolio with embossed front
cover; white paper insert with cut-out; color
post card; tape
Hadassah-Hebrew University Medical Center
c.1960s

04.015
Regional Meeting American Institute
of Planners, University Club,
Los Angeles, California
Black and white photographic print
Weaver LA
1950

05.031
Award: Honorary Life Membership to the
American Society of Planning Officials
Paper; black ink; ribbon; gold ink; gold seal;
glass; wood
American Society of Planning Officials
1964

06.004
Ladislas and Vilma Segoe
35mm color slide
Photographer unknown
c.1970s

PLANOGRAPHY: SELECTED PLANNING AND PLANNING RELATED STUDIES

1924 Cincinnati, Ohio — Statement and Evidence submitted on pending Zoning Ordinances

1925 Dayton, Ohio — Grade Crossing Elimination

1925 Cincinnati, Ohio — Official Plan

1926 Dayton, Ohio — A Comprehensive City Plan

1927 Louisville, Kentucky — Traffic Survey

1930 Dayton, Ohio and Its City Plan (Brochure)

1930 Covington, Kentucky and Environs — Comprehensive Plan

1931 Lexington (Kentucky) and Environs — Comprehensive Plan

1937 Our Cities — National Resources Committee

1939 Urban Planning & Land Policies — National Resources Committee

1939 Charleston and Environs, West Virginia — Comprehensive Plan

1939 Madison, Wisconsin — Comprehensive Plan

1942 Tucson (and Pima County) — Comprehensive Plan

1942 Tucson Regional Plan — Rehabilitation of Blighted Areas

1944 Piqua, Ohio — Master Plan

1945 Greenville, Ohio — Master Plan

1947 San Francisco, California — Redevelopment Study

1947 New City — San Francisco Redeveloped

1948 City of Detroit — Proposed Generalized Land Use Plan

1948 City of Detroit — Proposed Cultural Center Plan

1949 City of Detroit — Proposed Transportation Plan

1948 Cincinnati, Ohio — Metropolitan Master Plan

    1946. Riverfront Development Plan

    Cincinnati, Ohio — Master Plan Studies (Monographs)

    1945. Population

    1946. Airports

    1946. Economy of the Area

    1946. Industrial Areas

    1946. Public Transit

    1946. Residential Areas

    1946. Riverfront Development

    1947. Motorways

    1947. Parking

    1947. Public Service Facilities

    1947. Recreation

1948 San Francisco, California — Transportation Plan (with DeLeuw Cather)

1949 Chillicothe, Ohio — Master Plan

1950 Middletown, Ohio — Master Plan

1950 Richmond, Virginia — Master Plan

1950 Lexington, Kentucky — Master Plan

1951 Detroit, Michigan — Master Plan

    1945. Expressway and Transit System

    1945. Development of Riverfront, Master Plan (Brochure)

    1946. Recreational Facilities, Master Plan (Brochure)

    1946. Trafficways, Master Plan (Brochure)

    1947. Land Use Plan, Master Plan (Brochure)

1953 St. Albans, West Virginia — City Plan

1954 Hopkins, Minnesota — Master Plan

1956 South Charleston, West Virginia — City Plan

1956 Bellefontaine, Ohio — City Plan

1957 Rock Island, Illinois — Master Plan

1957 Oconomowoc, Wisconsin — City Plan

1957 Waukesha, Wisconsin — City Plan

1958 Rock Island Illinois — Extension of Comprehensive City Plan

1958 Cincinnati, Ohio — Zoning Ordinance Outline

1958 Lexington, Kentucky — Master Plan Supplement

1958 New Martinsville, West Virginia — City Plan

1958 Butler County, Ohio — Land Use Plan and Major Road Plan

1959 Ashland, Kentucky — Comprehensive Master Plan

1959 Hamilton, Ohio — Economic Feasibility Study

1959 Winona, Minnesota — Master Plan

1960 Chillicothe, Ohio — Master Plan (Revised)

1960 Rochester, Minnesota — Master Plan

1960 Zanesville, Ohio — Master Plan

1960 Flint, Michigan — Central Business District Plan and Comprehensive Master Plan

1960 Lansing, Michigan — Comprehensive Master Plan

1960 Watertown, Wisconsin — Comprehensive Master Plan

1961 Ohio County (Indiana) Planning Commission — Master Plan

1961 Columbus, Indiana — A Renewal Action Program

1961 Coshocton, Ohio — Comprehensive Master Plan

1962 Washington, Ohio — Comprehensive Master Plan

1962 Flint, Michigan — Comprehensive Master Plan

1962 Charleston, West Virginia — Revised Comprehensive Plan

1963 Mason, Ohio — Master Plan

1963 Tulsa, Oklahoma — Program for Community Renewal

1963 Bellaire, Ohio — Comprehensive Master Plan

1963 Huron, Ohio — Comprehensive Community Plan

1963 Heath, Ohio — Community Plan

1964 Ohio Master Plan — Fayette County

1964 Frederick, Maryland — Master Plan

1964 Delaware County, Ohio — Comprehensive Master Plan

1964 City of Delaware, Ohio — Comprehensive Master Plan

1964 Elmwood Place, Ohio — General Community Plan

1964 Granville, Ohio — Comprehensive Master Plan

1964 Guernsey County, Ohio — Comprehensive Master Plan

1964 St. Bernard, Ohio — General Community Plan

1964 Norwalk, Ohio — Comprehensive Master Plan

1964 Springfield, Missouri — Master Plan for Commercial Development

1964 Kanawha County, West Virginia — Comprehensive Metropolitan Plan

1964 Kanawha County, West Virginia — Plan Administration

1964 Kanawha County, West Virginia — Regional Traffic and Arterial Study

1964 Kenton, Ohio — Comprehensive Master Plan

1964 Newark, Ohio — Comprehensive Master Plan

1965 Lawrenceburg, Indiana — Comprehensive Master Plan

1965 Jasper, Indiana — Comprehensive Master Plan

1965 North College Hill, Ohio — Comprehensive Development Plan

1966 Fairfield, Ohio — Comprehensive Development Plan

1966 Franklin, Ohio — Comprehensive Development Plan

    1966. Report on Plan Effectuation and Review

    1966. Capital Improvements Program

1966 Comprehensive Development Plan, Reading Ohio

1966 Comprehensive Master Plan, Richmond, Indiana

1966 Comprehensive Master Plan, Wayne County, Indiana

1966 Comprehensive Master Plan, Cahokia, Illinois

1967 Comprehensive Master Plan, Aurora, Indiana

1971 Grant Park General Development and Land Use Plan

REFERENCES

1   **Birch, Eugenie Ladner**. "Practitioners and the Art of Planning, Journal of Planning Education and Research, Vol. 20, No. 4 (2001), pp. 407–422.

2   **Edelman, David J. and David J. Allor**. "Ladislas Segoe and the Emergence of the Professional Planning Consultant," Journal of Planning History, Vol. 2, No. 1 (February 2003), pp. 47–78.

3   **Edelman, David J., David J. Allor and April Smith**. 2000. *Ladislas Segoe and American Planning Practice*. Cincinnati: School of Planning, University of Cincinnati.

4   **Harper Brett**, 2001. *Ladislas and Vilma Segoe: A Visionary Couple and their Love for Life*. Cincinnati: The Ladislas and Vilma Segoe Family Foundation

5   **Krueckeberg, Donald A**. 1983. The American Planner: Biographies and Recollections. New York and London: Methuen.

6   **Roesler, W.G**. 1982. *Successful Urban Plans*. Lexington, MA and Toronto: Lexington Books, D.C. Heath.

POSTSCRIPT

IN THE PUBLIC INTEREST is an international collaboration that has involved many faculty, experts, and staff across the University of Cincinnati, Cornell University, and the Technion in Haifa, Israel. The project began in late 2012 when Professor of Planning, Dr. David J. Edelman, approached me about the feasibility of the two of us collaborating on a retrospective exhibition focused on the life and work of Ladislas Segoe, whose complete collection of professional and personal papers are housed at the UC Archives and Rare Books Library and at the Cornell University Archives.

I agreed that this project would be fun, interesting, and well-aligned with University priorities. I informed Dr. Edelman that an online exhibition (and eventually, a digital collection) would dovetail nicely with the vision of the University of Cincinnati Libraries, which has, under the progressive leadership of UC Libraries Dean, Xuemao Wang, turned its attention to the transformation of library research collections to enable new modes of scholarship.

With the help of Dr. Mark Carper, Dr. Edelman began the preliminary archival research at UC. We made meetings with UC Archivist and Head of the Archives and Rare Books Library, Kevin Grace, and Dr. Danilo Palazzo, Director of the UC/DAAP School of Planning, to discuss the logistics of our project such as our use of UC's archival materials in physical, traveling exhibitions, matters of digitization, the possibility of later digitizing the entire Segoe archive, and associated costs (and thankfully, Dr. Edelman had already secured funds from the Ladislas and Vilma Segoe Family Foundation through the good offices of one of its trustees, Mr. Lewis Gatch).

We then invited DAAP Assistant Professor of Architecture and Interior Design, Vincent Sansalone, to join our curatorial team as exhibition designer. The three of us, plus two graduate students, PhD candidate Jennifer Latessa, and MCP candidate Sara Woolf, both in the DAAP School of Planning, met frequently with several experts, specialists and faculty from around UC including Kevin Grace, Suzanne Maggard Reller, and Eira Tansey from the UC Archives and Rare Books Library; Holly Prochaska, Ashleigh Schieszer, and Jessica Ebert from the UC Preservation Lab; Nathan Tallman, UC Libraries Digital Collections Strategist; and Carolyn Hansen, UC Libraries Metadata Librarian.

Altogether, this group devised and executed the object, digitization, and exhibition strategies and began working on research, writing, object analysis, metadata, digitization, condition assessments, and object repair.

Finally, through the generous support of DAAP Dean, Robert Probst, we were able to bring yet another member of DAAP faculty on to the curatorial team, Assistant Professor of Graphic Communication Design, Todd Timney, without whose skills and dedication we would not have this professionally designed exhibition catalogue.

We hope that you enjoy the fruits of our efforts, which are indicative of the sort of organization the University of Cincinnati is: one that values creating and sharing knowledge acquired through thinking and working across the disciplines.

Jennifer Krivickas
Head of the Robert A. Deshon & Karl J. Schlachter Library for Design, Architecture, Art, and Planning (DAAP), University of Cincinnati